Maserati GranTurismo

MW01126244

More than 100 years after Maserati made its debut, the GranTurismo stuns drivers with its flashy looks and speed. From the trident that decorates the grille to the aerodynamic side skirts, this car was...

#2053741   E. Oachs   Available:01/01/2018   24 pgs
Grade:345 Dewey:629.2   AR:3.9 RC:5.2   LEX: 790

Porsche 911 Carrera $19.95

Since its debut in the 1960s, the Porsche 911 Carrera has been a shining star of the sports car world! Over the years, this popular vehicle has gone through many upgrades to keep it on top. A body made...

#2053742   E. Oachs   Available:01/01/2018   24 pgs
Grade:345 Dewey:629.22 AR:3.8 RC:4.5   LEX: 740

Tesla Model S $19.95

The Tesla Model S sets the benchmark for the future of cars! Not only does it run 100% on an electronic battery, but it has a system of sensitive cameras and sensors that allow it to safely drive itsel...

#2053743   E. Oachs   Available:01/01/2018   24 pgs
Grade:345 Dewey:629.2   AR:3.9 RC:4.6   LEX: 760

Aston Martin DB9 $19.95

Aston Martin supercars have celebrity status. Many models in the DB line have starred with British Secret Service Agent 007 in James Bond films. In this title, readers with a passion for cars will lear...

#1998180   E. Oachs   Available:01/01/2017   24 pgs
Grade:345 Dewey:629.22 AR:4.0 RC:4.7   LEX: 770

Chevrolet Camaro Z28 $19.95

With a top speed of more than 170 miles per hour, the Chevrolet Camaro Z/28 is a track star! It's also a veteran of the track, holding its own in races since the 1960s. Young readers, even those with s...

#1998181   E. Oachs   Available:01/01/2017   24 pgs
Grade:345 Dewey:629.22 AR:4.2 RC:5.3   LEX: 800

Dodge Challenger SRT Hellcat $19.95

Do you know why a Dodge Challenger SRT Hellcat comes with two car keys, one red and one black? Well, the black key is used when the full 707 horsepower would be too much to handle. Curious readers will...

#1998182 E. Oachs   Available:01/01/2017   24 pgs
Grade:345 Dewey:629.22 AR:4.2 RC:4.6   LEX: 760

Dodge Charger R/T $19.95

After years off the production line, the Dodge Charger R/T reappeared in 2005, in a much different form. The coupe of the 1960s became the sedan of today. In this book, young car enthusiasts can compar...

#1998183 E. Oachs   Available:01/01/2017   24 pgs
Grade:345 Dewey:629.22 AR:4.3 RC:5.3   LEX: 810

Ford Mustang Shelby GT350 $19.95

The Ford Mustang Shelby GT350 was named for its creator, Carroll Shelby. This American racecar driver of the 1950s designed this Ford model to maximize speed and power on the track. This hi-lo book hig...

#1998184 E. Oachs   Available:01/01/2017   24 pgs
Grade:345 Dewey:629.22 AR:4.1 RC:4.5   LEX: 740

Lykan HyperSport $19.95

The Lykan HyperSport is a car with a big price tag. It sells for more than $3 million! One reason for the high cost is that diamonds, sapphires, rubies, or emeralds are placed in the headlights. Young ...

#1998185 E. Oachs   Available:01/01/2017   24 pgs
Grade:345 Dewey:629.22 AR:4.1 RC:4.6   LEX: 760

Bentley Continental GT $19.95

This masterpiece is a perfect combination of classic Bentley and modern technology. Promising luxury and performance, the Bentley Continental GT will not disappoint. Uncover the secrets to creating cra...

#1923722 C. Cruz   Available:08/01/2015   24 pgs
Grade:345 Dewey:629.22 AR:4.1 RC:4.4   LEX: 720

JAGUAR
F-TYPE

BY NATHAN SOMMER

BELLWETHER MEDIA • MINNEAPOLIS, MN

Are you ready to take it to the extreme?
Torque books thrust you into the action-packed world
of sports, vehicles, mystery, and adventure. These books
may include dirt, smoke, fire, and dangerous stunts.
WARNING: read at your own risk.

This edition first published in 2020 by Bellwether Media, Inc.

No part of this publication may be reproduced in whole or in part without written permission of the publisher.
For information regarding permission, write to Bellwether Media, Inc., Attention: Permissions Department,
6012 Blue Circle Drive, Minnetonka, MN 55343.

Library of Congress Cataloging-in-Publication Data

Names: Sommer, Nathan, author.
Title: Jaguar F-Type / by Nathan Sommer.
Description: Minneapolis, MN : Bellwether Media, Inc., [2020] | Series:
   Torque. Car Crazy | Includes bibliographical references and index. |
   Audience: Age 7-12.
Identifiers: LCCN 2018057352 (print) | LCCN 2019004333 (ebook) | ISBN
   9781618915511 (ebook) | ISBN 9781644870105 (hardcover : alk. paper)
Subjects: LCSH: Jaguar F-type automobile–Juvenile literature.
Classification: LCC TL215.J3 (ebook) | LCC TL215.J3 S66 2020 (print) | DDC
   629.222/2–dc23
LC record available at https://lccn.loc.gov/2018057352

Editor: Kate Moening   Designer: Josh Brink

Printed in the United States of America, North Mankato, MN.

TABLE OF CONTENTS

A STUNNING RIDE

A Jaguar F-Type rounds the cliffs of a curvy mountain road. This **luxury** sports car is just as grand as the view next to it.

An outstanding **suspension system** keeps the ride smooth on the winding road. The F-Type was built to be safe and very fast!

The F-Type reaches a long, straight stretch. Now the car can really let loose! Its driver pushes a few buttons on the steering wheel. The car clicks into high gear.

The F-Type's engine roars as the car blasts straight ahead. Every ride in the Jaguar F-Type is an adventure!

THE HISTORY OF JAGUAR

Jaguar was founded by William Lyons and William Walmsley in 1922. It began as the Swallow Sidecar Company. The British company made parts for motorcycles.

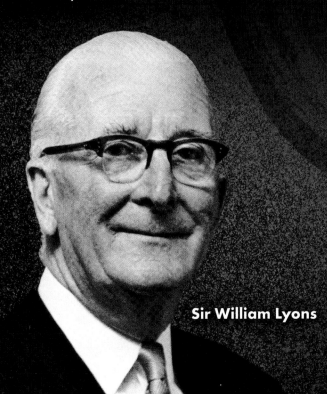

Sir William Lyons

CARS FIT FOR A QUEEN

IN 1956, QUEEN ELIZABETH II MADE WILLIAM LYONS A KNIGHT. THIS IS THE HIGHEST HONOR FOR A BRITISH CITIZEN! SIR LYONS' CAR COMPANY HAD MADE ENGLAND PROUD.

1936 SS Jaguar 2.5l Saloon

The Swallow Sidecar Company began making cars in the 1930s. Its first **model**, the SS Jaguar 2.5l Saloon, came out in 1935. Ten years later, Lyons decided to use the Jaguar name for the entire company!

Jaguar quickly made a name for itself with its winning sports cars. Its models won the **24 Hours of Le Mans** race five times in the 1950s.

**Jaguar D-Type at 1955
24 Hours of Le Mans**

BUILT TO WIN

THE C-TYPE IS JAGUAR'S MOST FAMOUS
RACE CAR. IT WAS RELEASED IN 1951.
THE CAR WON THE 24 HOURS OF LE MANS
ON ITS FIRST ATTEMPT!

Jaguar C-Type

Lyons aimed to make excellent cars
worth their price tag. Today, Jaguar cars
are popular worldwide.

JAGUAR F-TYPE

The F-Type was first shown as a **concept car** at the 2011 Frankfurt Motor Show. Its features and sleek appearance caught people's attention. The car won Best in Show at the event!

Jaguar F-Type concept car

READY FOR ANYTHING

JAGUAR CARRIED OUT MANY TESTS ON THE
F-TYPE BEFORE ITS RELEASE. THE COMPANY
TESTED THE CAR IN CONDITIONS AS COLD AS
-40 DEGREES FAHRENHEIT (-40 DEGREES CELSIUS)!

The F-Type blurs the line between sports cars
and everyday cars. It is the smallest car Jaguar
has made since 1954.

TECHNOLOGY AND GEAR

The F-Type comes as both a **coupe** and a **convertible**. Different F-Type models come with different engines. Some can go as fast as 200 miles (322 kilometers) per hour!

coupe

convertible

exhaust pipes

Some F-Type models have loud **exhaust pipes**. They make the F-Type roar like a race car!

The F-Type's **aluminum** body was built to create smooth **handling**. Its rear **spoiler** rises at high speeds to help the car grip the road. A front **splitter** directs air beneath the car. This helps the car move easily against the wind.

aluminum body

splitter

spoiler

JAGUAR

F-TYPE

Flat door handles blend in with the car's body. This helps the F-Type go even faster!

Inside, the F-Type is built like a race car. Its ultra-light seats give support at high speeds. The seats can even be heated or cooled for the most comfortable ride possible!

A 10-inch (25-centimeter) touch screen comes with **GPS navigation**. The touch screen also lets drivers control the car's temperature and lighting color.

touch screen

2019 F-TYPE SVR COUPE SPECIFICATIONS

CAR STYLE	COUPE
ENGINE	5.0L V8
TOP SPEED	200 MILES (322 KILOMETERS) PER HOUR
0 - 60 TIME	3.5 SECONDS
HORSEPOWER	575 HP (429 KILOWATTS) @ 6,500 RPM
CURB WEIGHT	UP TO 3,874 POUNDS (1,757 KILOGRAMS)
WIDTH	80.4 INCHES (203 CENTIMETERS)
LENGTH	176 INCHES (448 CENTIMETERS)
HEIGHT	51.6 INCHES (131 CENTIMETERS)
WHEEL SIZE	20 INCHES (51 CENTIMETERS)
COST	STARTS AT $122,750

TODAY AND THE FUTURE

Jaguar plans to make even more sports cars in the future. But the company will keep the F-Type as the face of its brand. Jaguar may even work with the BMW car company to give the car a more powerful engine.

The F-Type turns heads wherever it goes. It is a truly amazing ride!

HOW TO SPOT A JAGUAR F-TYPE

FLAT DOOR HANDLES   **REAR SPOILER**   **FRONT SPLITTER**

GLOSSARY

24 Hours of Le Mans—a race in which a team of drivers competes for 24 hours

aluminum—a strong, lightweight metal

concept car—a car made to highlight new styles or technology; concept cars are not usually for sale.

convertible—a car with a folding or soft roof

coupe—a car with a hard roof and two doors

exhaust pipes—pipes used to direct gases from a car's engine out of the engine and away from the car

GPS navigation—a car system that provides maps and directions to get around

handling—how a car performs around turns

luxury—expensive and offering great comfort

model—a specific kind of car

splitter—a flat scoop under the front bumper that makes a car more aerodynamic

spoiler—a part on the back of the car that helps the car grip the road

suspension system—a series of springs and shocks that help a car grip the road

TO LEARN MORE

AT THE LIBRARY

Lanier, Wendy Hinote. *Sports Cars*. Lake Elmo, Minn.: Focus Readers, 2017.

Mason, Paul. *British Supercars: McLaren, Aston Martin, Jaguar*. New York, N.Y.: PowerKids Press, 2019.

Oachs, Emily Rose. *Aston Martin DB9*. Minneapolis, Minn.: Bellwether Media, 2017.

ON THE WEB

FACTSURFER

Factsurfer.com gives you a safe, fun way to find more information.

1. Go to www.factsurfer.com.

2. Enter "Jaguar F-Type" into the search box and click 🔍.

3. Select your book cover to see a list of related web sites.

INDEX

Bugatti Veyron $19.95

Ettore Bugatti's company has created some of the finest hand-built cars for the roads around the world. The Bugatti Veyron's sleek design is meant to enhance its powerful performance. Keep up with Buga...

#1923723   C. Cruz   Available:08/01/2015   24 pgs
Grade:345   Dewey:629.22   AR:3.8   RC:3.8   LEX: 750

Chevrolet Corvette Z06 $19.95

The Chevrolet Corvette Z06 holds its own in the world of sports cars. Ranked among the most elite in its category, this car can keep up with the rest. Check out America's favorite sports car in this ad...

#1923724   C. Cruz   Available:08/01/2015   24 pgs
Grade:345   Dewey:629.22   AR:4.1   RC:4.6   LEX: 750

Dodge Viper SRT $19.95

Start your Dodge Viper SRT engine! With one of the most powerful engines on the planet, this car will bring your automotive emotions to a new high. Learn about this successful car brand in this engagin...

#1923725   C. Cruz   Available:08/01/2015   24 pgs
Grade:345   Dewey:629.22   AR:4.0   RC:4.5   LEX: 730

Ferrari 458 Italia $19.95

The racetrack has heavily influenced many Ferrari car designs. The Ferrari 458 Italia is a road car with major racing abilities. It can reach speeds of more than 200 miles per hour! Buckle up for this ...

#1923726   C. Cruz   Available:08/01/2015   24 pgs
Grade:345   Dewey:629.22   AR:4.0   RC:4.4   LEX: 720

Lamborghini Aventador $19.95

The Lamborghini Aventador LP 700-4 is at the top of its class when it comes to performance. This car has the strongest engine ever built by Lamborghini and accelerates from 0 to 62 miles per hour in le...

#1923727   C. Cruz   Available:08/01/2015   24 pgs
Grade:345   Dewey:629.22   AR:3.8   RC:4.3   LEX: 690